I AM MY *Beloved's*

Celebrating Passion and Intimacy in Your Marriage

THE SONG OF SOLOMON

with selected quotes by

Dennis Rainey and Tommy Nelson

THOMAS NELSON PUBLISHERS
Nashville

Presented to:

_____

From:

_____

Date:

_____

The Song of Solomon is the number one song of all the songs written by the wisest man who ever lived. Add to that the seal of the Holy Spirit of God! This is a magnificent book inspired by God and placed in the Scriptures with elegance, beauty, and dignity. Every time I read it, I receive a spiritual wheel alignment in the areas of love, romance, and passion.

Dennis Rainey

Because of the nature of our day, we have lost touch with God our Creator, and we have lost touch with what He has created us to be. We do not understand marriage, commitment, romance, sex, or intimacy. Without God these are merely biological functions and happy notions. But God has told us very clearly in His Word about the institution of marriage and the delightful gift of sexual intimacy within marriage. Discover through the Song of Solomon that these are indeed God's wonderful creations and bountiful gifts!

Tommy Nelson

CONTENTS

PASSION, FIRE, ROMANCE...

As she passed by, the folds of her long skirt gently brushed against his leg. Her scent lingered in the air. And with one demure glance she looked back.

His eyes locked on hers.

The moment froze in eternity—an instant knowing, understanding—without a word spoken. The world around them, once buzzing with conversation, was silenced now by the passion ignited through one glance. Every other man in the room wondered what secret he knew; every other woman felt pangs of envy. Those two had it: Passion. Fire. Romance.

And, after 15 years of marriage, it was hotter than ever.

Their secret? What the Bible had taught for thousands of years.

Solomon, the wisest man who ever lived, knew this kind of passion. He lived it, loved it, and captured it in song.

Of the 1005 songs Solomon wrote, the one dubbed "Song of Songs"—his number one hit single—was about this passionate love. And romance. And sex. And God.

Though some Christians think God doesn't belong in the bedroom, Solomon welcomed Him in. With God's blessing, he and his wife experienced the most intimate union of flesh and spirit, a physical chemistry born of the deepest understanding of their spiritual and emotional needs.

Using a variety of literary devices, Solomon reveals the depth of love between his wife, the Shulamite woman—the love of his life—and himself, the beloved. Through the comments of the Daughters of Jerusalem, the Shulamite's attendants, Solomon narrates the intensity of their passionate love as it progresses through dating, courtship, marriage, and maturity. And at a key moment in the love story, God Himself steps in with favor and approval—encouraging the couple to enjoy the gift He's given them.

How exciting that the God who created us with a capacity to feel and experience such depth of emotion is both the foremost expert on our need for romance and the designer of marriage! How exciting, too, that the God who intended His people to live with the joy and intensity of such satisfaction

didn't leave us without directions on how to achieve it.
In fact, He dedicated an entire book of the Bible to the subject
just so we could understand.

With God as the unifying bond, man and woman can know
an intimacy and wholeness that only sweetens with time. And
while the flirtations of courtship and the giddiness of young
love come and go, the roots of companionship grow ever
deeper and stronger over time.

So open God's Word and see passion through His eyes. Discover with us the most romantic love story ever told—right in the heart of Scripture. And see how the Song of Solomon unashamedly answers the cry of us all for sexual and spiritual wholeness.

It's not a secret any more. Passion, fire, and romance in marriage . . . can be fully yours!

intimacy

God's design for marital love includes bountiful romance and passion built on a foundation of commitment, communication, and intimacy. True intimacy thrives in the fertile environment of dynamic spiritual commitment and a lifelong marriage covenant.

Dennis Rainey

Spiritual Commitment

The song of songs, which *is* Solomon's.

The Banquet

THE SHULAMITE

Let him kiss me with the kisses of his mouth—
For your love *is* better than wine.
Because of the fragrance of your good ointments,
Your name *is* ointment poured forth;
Therefore the virgins love you.
Draw me away!

THE DAUGHTERS OF JERUSALEM
We will run after you.

THE SHULAMITE
The king has brought me into his chambers.

THE DAUGHTERS OF JERUSALEM
We will be glad and rejoice in you.

We will remember your love more than wine.

The Shulamite

Rightly do they love you.

I *am* dark, but lovely,
O daughters of Jerusalem,
Like the tents of Kedar,
Like the curtains of Solomon.
Do not look upon me, because I *am* dark,
Because the sun has tanned me.

My mother's sons were angry with me;
They made me the keeper of the vineyards,
But my own vineyard I have not kept.

(TO HER BELOVED)

Tell me, O you whom I love,
Where you feed *your flock,*
Where you make *it* rest at noon.
For why should I be as one who veils herself
By the flocks of your companions?

The Beloved

If you do not know, O fairest among women,
Follow in the footsteps of the flock,
And feed your little goats
Beside the shepherds' tents.
I have compared you, my love,
To my filly among Pharaoh's chariots.
Your cheeks are lovely with ornaments,
Your neck with chains *of gold*.

It's a wise woman who knows how to please her husband in a way that enflames his soul for her. One of the reasons we marry is to enjoy passionate love with another! Unfortunately, the day-to-day routines of life can dampen this "fire," intimacy, and romance. To keep the "home fires" of romance and passion burning, feed the "fire" with the fuel of focused attention, time, and conversation.

Dennis Rainey

THE DAUGHTERS OF JERUSALEM

We will make you ornaments of gold
With studs of silver.

THE SHULAMITE

While the king *is* at his table,
My spikenard sends forth its fragrance.
A bundle of myrrh *is* my beloved to me,

That lies all night between my breasts.
My beloved *is* to me a cluster of henna *blooms*
In the vineyards of En Gedi.

THE BELOVED

Behold, you *are* fair, my love!
Behold, you *are* fair!
You *have* dove's eyes.

The Shulamite

Behold, you *are* handsome, my beloved!
Yes, pleasant!
Also our bed *is* green.
The beams of our houses *are* cedar,
And our rafters of fir.
I *am* the rose of Sharon,
And the lily of the valleys.

When we take a wife to be our beloved, our darling, our lover, we set her apart and put her on a pedestal. We say, "I chose you out of all the women in the world to be my bride, my queen—a person of worth, value, and dignity whom I will care for and cherish."

Dennis Rainey

DIGNITY

The Beloved

Like a lily among thorns,
So is my love among the daughters.

The Shulamite

Like an apple tree among the trees of the woods,
So *is* my beloved among the sons.
I sat down in his shade with great delight,
And his fruit *was* sweet to my taste.

THE SHULAMITE TO THE DAUGHTERS OF JERUSALEM

He brought me to the banqueting house,
And his banner over me *was* love.
Sustain me with cakes of raisins,
Refresh me with apples,
For I *am* lovesick.

His left hand *is* under my head,
And his right hand embraces me.
I charge you, O daughters of Jerusalem,
By the gazelles or by the does of the field,
Do not stir up nor awaken love
Until it pleases.

The Beloved's Request

THE SHULAMITE

The voice of my beloved!
Behold, he comes
Leaping upon the mountains,
Skipping upon the hills.
My beloved is like a gazelle or a young stag.
Behold, he stands behind our wall;
He is looking through the windows,
Gazing through the lattice.

Communicate to your husband your admiration and respect by spoken affirmations: Tell him that you appreciate his character, admire his obedience to Christ, and proudly wear his good name. When a wife lists the specific admirable qualities of her husband, her words massage him with love. And with her encouragement he will become an even better man.

Dennis Rainey

My beloved spoke, and said to me:
"Rise up, my love, my fair one,
And come away.
For lo, the winter is past,
The rain is over *and* gone.
The flowers appear on the earth;
The time of singing has come,

And the voice of the turtledove
Is heard in our land.
The fig tree puts forth her green figs,
And the vines *with* the tender grapes
Give a good smell.
Rise up, my love, my fair one,
And come away!

"O my dove, in the clefts of the rock,
In the secret *places* of the cliff,
Let me see your face,
Let me hear your voice;
For your voice *is* sweet,
And your face *is* lovely."

Her Brothers

Catch us the foxes,
The little foxes that spoil the vines,
For our vines *have* tender grapes.

The Shulamite

My beloved *is* mine, and I *am* his.
He feeds *his flock* among the lilies.

Choose to remain absolutely faithful to your spouse. Choose to focus on the inner qualities of your spouse and to nurture, edify, and praise them. Choose to recall frequently the things that you admire in your spouse and to recall special moments that have enriched your relationship through the years. Choose to make the effort to show your spouse frequently how much you love, honor, and cherish them.

Tommy Nelson

(TO HER BELOVED)

    Until the day breaks
    And the shadows flee away,
    Turn, my beloved,
    And be like a gazelle
    Or a young stag
    Upon the mountains of Bether.

A Troubled Night

THE SHULAMITE

By night on my bed I sought the one I love;
I sought him, but I did not find him.
"I will rise now," *I said,*
"And go about the city;
In the streets and in the squares
I will seek the one I love."

I sought him, but I did not find him.
The watchmen who go about the city found me;
I said,
"Have you seen the one I love?"

Scarcely had I passed by them,
When I found the one I love.
I held him and would not let him go,

Until I had brought him to the house of my mother,
And into the chamber of her who conceived me.

I charge you, O daughters of Jerusalem,
By the gazelles or by the does of the field,
Do not stir up nor awaken love
Until it pleases.

One of the supreme joys of marriage is to know
and be known intimately by another. Married love is
an oasis, a haven of refreshment and nourishment
for weary souls amid life's desert.

Dennis Rainey

The Coming of Solomon

THE SHULAMITE

Who *is* this coming out of the wilderness
Like pillars of smoke,
Perfumed with myrrh and frankincense,
With all the merchant's fragrant powders?

Behold, it *is* Solomon's couch,
With sixty valiant men around it,
Of the valiant of Israel.
They all hold swords,
Being expert in war.
Every man *has* his sword on his thigh
Because of fear in the night.

Of the wood of Lebanon
Solomon the King
Made himself a palanquin:
He made its pillars of silver,
Its support of gold,
Its seat of purple,

Its interior paved *with* love
By the daughters of Jerusalem.
Go forth, O daughters of Zion,
And see King Solomon with the crown
With which his mother crowned him
On the day of his wedding,
The day of the gladness of his heart.

It is imperative that a husband understands his wife's greatest romantic need: to be spiritually led and protected by her man. I believe every woman absolutely relishes the thought that she has a man willing to serve as a protector of her soul by sensing her spiritual needs, by standing beside her, and by interceding on her behalf.

Dennis Rainey

SPIRITUAL NEEDS

The Bridegroom Praises the Bride

THE BELOVED

Behold, you *are* fair, my love!
Behold, you *are* fair!
You *have* dove's eyes behind your veil.
Your hair *is* like a flock of goats,
Going down from Mount Gilead.
Your teeth *are* like a flock of shorn *sheep*

Which have come up from the washing,
Every one of which bears twins,
And none *is* barren among them.
Your lips *are* like a strand of scarlet,
And your mouth is lovely.
Your temples behind your veil
Are like a piece of pomegranate.

Your neck *is* like the tower of David,
Built for an armory,
On which hang a thousand bucklers,
All shields of mighty men.
Your two breasts *are* like two fawns,
Twins of a gazelle,
Which feed among the lilies.

Until the day breaks
And the shadows flee away,
I will go my way to the mountain of myrrh
And to the hill of frankincense.

You *are* all fair, my love,
And *there is* no spot in you.
Come with me from Lebanon, *my* spouse,
With me from Lebanon.

A wife's sexual response to her husband is rooted
in her respect for his character—his good name, his
integrity, his kindness. Emotional trust and commitment
are the embers from which leaps the blaze of physical
passion between a husband and wife.

Dennis Rainey

emotional trust

Look from the top of Amana,
From the top of Senir and Hermon,
From the lions' dens,
From the mountains of the leopards.

You have ravished my heart,
My sister, *my* spouse;
You have ravished my heart
With one *look* of your eyes,

With one link of your necklace.
How fair is your love,
My sister, *my* spouse!
How much better than wine is your love,
And the scent of your perfumes
Than all spices!
Your lips, O *my* spouse,
Drip as the honeycomb;

Honey and milk *are* under your tongue;
And the fragrance of your garments
Is like the fragrance of Lebanon.

A garden enclosed
Is my sister, *my* spouse,
A spring shut up,
A fountain sealed.

Your plants *are* an orchard of pomegranates
With pleasant fruits,
Fragrant henna with spikenard,
Spikenard and saffron,
Calamus and cinnamon,
With all trees of frankincense,
Myrrh and aloes,
With all the chief spices—

When sexual intimacy occurs in right timing and with the right person, from God's perspective, it is meant to be enjoyed fully. Once you are with your beloved and within the vows of holy matrimony, sex is meant to be a source of pleasure for both the man and woman.

Tommy Nelson

A fountain of gardens,
A well of living waters,
And streams from Lebanon.

THE SHULAMITE
Awake, O north *wind*,
And come, O south!
Blow upon my garden,
That its spices may flow out.
Let my beloved come to his garden
And eat its pleasant fruits.

THE BELOVED

I have come to my garden, my sister, *my* spouse;
I have gathered my myrrh with my spice;
I have eaten my honeycomb with my honey;
I have drunk my wine with my milk.

GOD

Eat, O friends!
Drink, yes, drink deeply,
O beloved ones!

The Shulamite's Troubled Evening

THE SHULAMITE

I sleep, but my heart is awake;
It is the voice of my beloved!
He knocks, *saying,*
"Open for me, my sister, my love,
My dove, my perfect one;
For my head is covered with dew,
My locks with the drops of the night."

I have taken off my robe;
How can I put it on *again?*
I have washed my feet;
How can I defile them?
My beloved put his hand
By the latch *of the door,*
And my heart yearned for him.

Those who are faithfully committed in marriage regard their marriage as their most precious possession— a genuine treasure. Hold tightly to the precious gift you have been given. Don't allow yourself to become casual or nonchalant about your marriage.

Tommy Nelson

I arose to open for my beloved,
And my hands dripped *with* myrrh,
My fingers with liquid myrrh,
On the handles of the lock.

I opened for my beloved,
But my beloved had turned away *and* was gone.
My heart leaped up when he spoke.
I sought him, but I could not find him;

I called him, but he gave me no answer.
The watchmen who went about the city found me.
They struck me, they wounded me;
The keepers of the walls
Took my veil away from me.
I charge you, O daughters of Jerusalem,
If you find my beloved,
That you tell him I *am* lovesick!

THE DAUGHTERS OF JERUSALEM

What *is* your beloved
More than *another* beloved,
O fairest among women?
What *is* your beloved
More than *another* beloved,
That you so charge us?

THE SHULAMITE

My beloved *is* white and ruddy,
Chief among ten thousand.

His head *is like* the finest gold;
His locks *are* wavy,
And black as a raven.
His eyes *are* like doves
By the rivers of waters,
Washed with milk,
And fitly set.
His cheeks *are* like a bed of spices,
Banks of scented herbs.
His lips *are* lilies,
Dripping liquid myrrh.

Romance is about giving to another person. It is about appreciating that person and valuing that person. It is about showing signs of respect and trust. It is about admiration.

Tommy Nelson

RESPECT

His hands *are* rods of gold
Set with beryl.
His body *is* carved ivory
Inlaid *with* sapphires.
His legs *are* pillars of marble
Set on bases of fine gold.
His countenance *is* like Lebanon,
Excellent as the cedars.

His mouth *is* most sweet,
Yes, he *is* altogether lovely.
This *is* my beloved,
And this *is* my friend,
O daughters of Jerusalem!

The Daughters of Jerusalem

Where has your beloved gone,
O fairest among women?
Where has your beloved turned aside,
That we may seek him with you?

THE SHULAMITE

My beloved has gone to his garden,
To the beds of spices,
To feed *his flock* in the gardens,
And to gather lilies.
I *am* my beloved's,
And my beloved *is* mine.
He feeds *his flock* among the lilies.

Praise of the Shulamite's Beauty

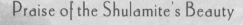

THE BELOVED
O my love, you *are as* beautiful as Tirzah,
Lovely as Jerusalem,
Awesome as *an army* with banners!
Turn your eyes away from me,
For they have overcome me.

Show me a woman who feels that her husband deals with

her tenderly—with kindness, good manners, generosity, genuine

affection, and understanding—and I'll show you a happily married

woman, regardless of external circumstances that may come against

their union or family. Show me a husband who feels that his wife

deals with him with respect—admiration, appreciation, upholding

his dignity as a man, thankful for his protection and provision—

and I'll show you a happily married man, regardless

of the stress he may feel from the outside world.

Tommy Nelson

Your hair *is* like a flock of goats
Going down from Gilead.
Your teeth *are* like a flock of sheep
Which have come up from the washing;
Every one bears twins,
And none *is* barren among them.
Like a piece of pomegranate
Are your temples behind your veil.

There are sixty queens
And eighty concubines,
And virgins without number.
My dove, my perfect one,
Is the only one,
The only one of her mother,
The favorite of the one who bore her.

The daughters saw her
And called her blessed,
The queens and the concubines,
And they praised her.

Who is she who looks forth as the morning,
Fair as the moon,
Clear as the sun,
Awesome as *an army* with banners?

THE SHULAMITE

I went down to the garden of nuts
To see the verdure of the valley,
To see whether the vine had budded
And the pomegranates had bloomed.
Before I was even aware,
My soul had made me
As the chariots of my noble people.

Romance requires intention, care, and focus. It requires that each person keep in active memory what gave birth to the marriage. It requires that each person continue to remember the special traits in the spouse that fueled attraction at the initial stages of their relationship. Love must be shown. Honor must be expressed. Cherish is an attitude that must be displayed. Passionate marriages are so by design and intent. Romance is a discipline.

Tommy Nelson

The Beloved and His Friends

Return, return, O Shulamite;
Return, return, that we may look upon you!

The Shulamite

What would you see in the Shulamite—
As it were, the dance of the two camps?

Expressions of Praise

THE BELOVED

How beautiful are your feet in sandals,
O prince's daughter!
The curves of your thighs *are* like jewels,
The work of the hands of a skillful workman.
Your navel *is* a rounded goblet;

It lacks no blended beverage.
Your waist *is* a heap of wheat
Set about with lilies.
Your two breasts *are* like two fawns,
Twins of a gazelle.
Your neck *is* like an ivory tower,
Your eyes *like* the pools in Heshbon
By the gate of Bath Rabbim.

Your nose *is* like the tower of Lebanon
Which looks toward Damascus.
Your head *crowns* you like *Mount* Carmel,
And the hair of your head *is* like purple;
A king *is* held captive by *your* tresses.

How fair and how pleasant you are,
O love, with your delights!

This stature of yours is like a palm tree,
And your breasts *like* its clusters.
I said, "I will go up to the palm tree,
I will take hold of its branches."
Let now your breasts be like clusters of the vine,
The fragrance of your breath like apples,
And the roof of your mouth like the best wine.

A Christian man and wife ought to have the most passionate, sensual relationship. Jesus Christ cleanses their consciences, and they have fellowship with God and with one another in the way their Maker designed. Their union is blessed and sealed by God. The passion flowing between them should be holy and electrifying!

Dennis Rainey

THE SHULAMITE

The wine goes *down* smoothly for my beloved,
Moving gently the lips of sleepers.
I *am* my beloved's,
And his desire *is* toward me.

Come, my beloved,
Let us go forth to the field;
Let us lodge in the villages.
Let us get up early to the vineyards;

Let us see if the vine has budded,
Whether the grape blossoms are open,
And the pomegranates are in bloom.
There I will give you my love.
The mandrakes give off a fragrance,
And at our gates *are* pleasant *fruits*,
All manner, new and old,

Which I have laid up for you, my beloved.
Oh, that you were like my brother,
Who nursed at my mother's breasts!
If I should find you outside,
I would kiss you;
I would not be despised.

Sex is a sacred, mystical union of a groom and his bride. God gave sex to us for pleasure, for oneness in body, soul, and spirit, and as a means of bearing children. There should be a sense of reverence for something so intimate and majestic. We need God's perspective on a subject that is so tainted and twisted in our culture. That's why the Song of Solomon needs to be read, reflected upon, and applied to our marriage relationships.

Dennis Rainey

I would lead you *and* bring you
Into the house of my mother,
She *who* used to instruct me.
I would cause you to drink of spiced wine,
Of the juice of my pomegranate.

(TO THE DAUGHTERS OF JERUSALEM)
His left hand *is* under my head,
And his right hand embraces me.
I charge you, O daughters of Jerusalem,
Do not stir up nor awaken love
Until it pleases.

Love Renewed in Lebanon

A RELATIVE

Who *is* this coming up from the wilderness,
Leaning upon her beloved?

I awakened you under the apple tree.
There your mother brought you forth;
There she *who* bore you brought *you* forth.

The Shulamite to Her Beloved

Set me as a seal upon your heart,
As a seal upon your arm;
For love *is as* strong as death,
Jealousy *as* cruel as the grave;
Its flames *are* flames of fire,
A most vehement flame.

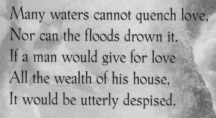

Many waters cannot quench love,
Nor can the floods drown it.
If a man would give for love
All the wealth of his house,
It would be utterly despised.

THE SHULAMITE'S BROTHERS

We have a little sister,
And she has no breasts.

In God's plan for marriage, the romance continues throughout the marriage. In fact, it builds and grows into a loving and passionate marriage that is even more wonderful in its latter stages than in its beginning.

Tommy Nelson

What shall we do for our sister
In the day when she is spoken for?
If she *is* a wall,
We will build upon her
A battlement of silver;
And if she *is* a door,
We will enclose her
With boards of cedar.

The Shulamite

I *am* a wall,
And my breasts like towers;
Then I became in his eyes
As one who found peace.
Solomon had a vineyard at Baal Hamon;
He leased the vineyard to keepers;
Everyone was to bring for its fruit
A thousand silver coins.

(To Solomon)

> My own vineyard *is* before me.
> You, O Solomon, *may have* a thousand,
> And those who tend its fruit two hundred.

The Beloved

> You who dwell in the gardens,
> The companions listen for your voice—
> Let me hear it!

The Shulamite

Make haste, my beloved,
And be like a gazelle
Or a young stag
On the mountains of spices.

$\mathcal{G}$od desires for you to experience the fullness of joy
made possible through love, sexual intimacy, and romance.
Trust God to help you find and develop a relationship
that is anchored in Him. And then enjoy to the
maximum His wonderful gift to you!

Tommy Nelson

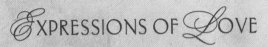

EXPRESSIONS OF LOVE

Words have the power to bring either life or death. You can strengthen your love relationship with your mate by speaking gracious words that affirm and edify. Express words of love and commitment to your mate here:

_____

_____

_____

_____

_____

_____

_____

Dennis Rainey and the FamilyLife team have created a number of practical, Christ-centered resources for couples:

- FamilyLife Marriage Conferences
- "FamilyLife Today," their nationally syndicated radio broadcast
- *My Lover, My Friend* audio series
- *Moments Together for Couples*, Dennis and Barbara Rainey's best-selling book

For these and other resources, visit FamilyLife's Web site at www.familylife.com or call them at 1-800-FL-TODAY.

Tommy Nelson's quotes are taken from his newly released title, *The Book of Romance*, which is based on his teaching series entitled "The Song of Solomon: A Study of Love, Sex, Marriage, and Romance." To purchase a copy of *The Book of Romance*, visit your local bookstore. For information on:

- attending a Song of Solomon Conference by Tommy Nelson
- purchasing the video or audio teaching series on the Song of Solomon
- or other teaching material by Tommy Nelson

contact Hudson Productions at 1-800-729-0815, visit their Web site at www.thesongofsolomon.com, or write to them at 12001 North Central Expressway, Suite 150, Box 120, Dallas, TX 75243.